SPACE SCIENCE

THE MOON

BY NATHAN SOMMER

BELLWETHER MEDIA ∘ MINNEAPOLIS, MN

TM

Are you ready to take it to the extreme? Torque books thrust you into the action-packed world of sports, vehicles, mystery, and adventure. These books may include dirt, smoke, fire, and chilling tales. **WARNING**: read at your own risk.

This edition first published in 2019 by Bellwether Media, Inc.

No part of this publication may be reproduced in whole or in part without written permission of the publisher.
For information regarding permission, write to Bellwether Media, Inc.,
Attention: Permissions Department,
6012 Blue Circle Drive, Minnetonka, MN 55343.

Library of Congress Cataloging-in-Publication Data

Names: Sommer, Nathan, author.
Title: The Moon / by Nathan Sommer.
Description: Minneapolis, MN : Bellwether Media, Inc., [2019] | Series:
   Torque. Space Science | Audience: Ages 7-12. | Audience: Grades 3 to 7. |
   Includes bibliographical references and index.
Identifiers: LCCN 2018039176 (print) | LCCN 2018040670 (ebook) | ISBN
   9781681036939 (ebook) | ISBN 9781626179752 (hardcover : alk. paper)
Subjects: LCSH: Moon–Juvenile literature.
Classification: LCC QB582 (ebook) | LCC QB582 .S66 2019 (print) | DDC
   523.3–dc23
LC record available at https://lccn.loc.gov/2018039176

Editor: Kate Moening   Designer: Andrea Schneider

Printed in the United States of America, North Mankato, MN.

TABLE OF CONTENTS

THE ECLIPSE OF A LIFETIME

It is July 27, 2018. A crowd gathers to see the **lunar eclipse** in the night sky. The Moon appears a bold red.

A lunar eclipse happens when Earth crosses between the Moon and Sun. Earth's **atmosphere** bends sunlight. This makes the light look red when it reaches the Moon. These rare eclipses are not to be missed!

FUN FACT

COLOR-CHANGING MOON

Because of its reddish color, the lunar eclipse is sometimes called a "blood moon"!

WHAT IS THE MOON?

The Moon is Earth's only natural **satellite**. It is only about a fourth of Earth's size! The satellite circles Earth about once every 27 days.

The Moon can get both very hot and very cold. It reaches 253 degrees Fahrenheit (123 degrees Celsius) in some places. It gets as cold as -414 degrees Fahrenheit (-248 degrees Celsius) in others!

**EARTH VS. MOON
SIZE COMPARISON**

FUN FACT

GOODBYE, MOON!

The Moon is slowly distancing itself from Earth. Each year, it moves about 1.5 inches (3.8 centimeters) away!

The Moon has a very thin atmosphere. It gets hit by many **asteroids** as a result. The asteroids leave mountains and large **craters** across the Moon's surface.

The Moon's **gravity** causes regular rises and falls in the Earth's sea levels. These are called tides. The Moon's gravity also slows Earth's **rotation** over time.

CRATER

THE MOON'S
SURFACE

The Moon has a light **core** and thick **crust**. Without an atmosphere, it has no weather. Piles of dust sit unmoved for hundreds of years! There are also no seasons on the Moon. Most of the satellite never gets any sunlight. It is cold, dusty, and dark.

FUN FACT

A QUIET PLACE

Because of the lack of atmosphere, no sound can be heard on the Moon. It also makes its sky look black!

HOW DID THE MOON FORM?

The Moon likely formed 100 million years after the planets formed. Many scientists believe it was created when a large object crashed into Earth. This caused a piece of the planet to break off into **orbit**.

Volcanoes rocked the Moon's surface for millions of years. **Magma** bubbled up from the ground. This formed the satellite's dusty, rocky surface.

FUN FACT

MOONQUAKES

Sudden, violent quakes shake the Moon's surface today. Most of these are caused by gravity's pull between Earth, the Sun, and the Moon.

ILLUSTRATION OF THE
MOON FORMING

WHERE IS THE MOON FOUND?

The Moon is on average 238,855 miles (384,400 kilometers) away from Earth. Because its orbit is oval-shaped, it is sometimes closer or farther away.

Perigee is the point where the Moon is as close to Earth as possible. Sometimes, perigee results in a **supermoon**. During a supermoon, the Moon appears larger and brighter than ever!

HOW FAR AWAY IS THE MOON?

EARTH TO MOON = 238,855 MILES
(384,400 KILOMETERS)

What we see of the Moon depends on how much sunlight strikes it. It has four different **phases** when viewed from Earth. The phases change as the Moon and Sun move through space.

Only one side of the Moon can ever be seen from Earth. This is because the Moon rotates at the same speed it orbits the planet.

PHASES OF THE MOON

NEW MOON

FULL MOON

FIRST QUARTER

LAST QUARTER

WHY DO WE STUDY THE MOON?

The Moon was the first object in space humans set foot on. Scientists want to see if the satellite can house a future space lab.

The Moon's surface has hundreds of deep pits. Scientists believe these pits are safe from asteroids and temperature changes. They could be where **astronauts** learn to live and work in space.

FUN FACT

THE FIRST MOONWALK

In 1969, Neil Armstrong became the first human to walk on the Moon. The United States astronaut is one of just twelve ever to do so!

19

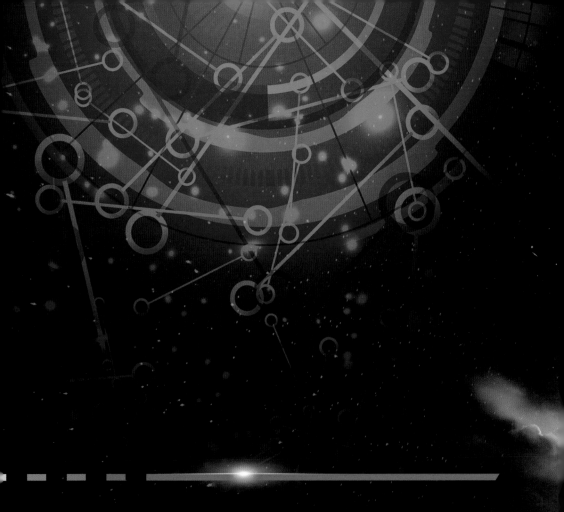

The surfaces of Earth and the Moon used to look alike. While Earth's surface changed over time, the Moon's mostly stayed the same. Studying its surface can tell us about Earth's past. It can also help scientists understand how Earth has changed.

The surface of the Moon may stay the same, but its future is alive with endless possibilities!

GLOSSARY

asteroids–small rocky objects that orbit the Sun

astronauts–scientists who explore and study space

atmosphere–the gases that surround a planet

core–the innermost part of the Moon

craters–deep holes in the surface of an object

crust–the uppermost part of the Moon's surface

gravity–the force that pulls objects toward one another

lunar eclipse–an event in which Earth moves between the Moon and Sun

magma–hot fluid that shoots up from a planet's or satellite's surface to create lava

orbit–a complete movement around something in a fixed pattern

phases–different appearances the Moon has when viewed from Earth, depending on how much sunlight is striking it

rotation–the turning of an object on its axis

satellite–an object that orbits planets and asteroids

supermoon–when a full moon occurs during perigee; the Moon looks noticeably brighter and larger during supermoons.

volcanoes–vents that let out hot rocks and steam

TO LEARN MORE

AT THE LIBRARY

DeYoe, Aaron. *Space Travel*. Minneapolis, Minn.: Super Sandcastle, 2016.

Mahoney, Emily. *What Is On the Far Side of the Moon?*. New York, N.Y.: Gareth Stevens Publishing, 2019.

Morey, Allan. *Lunar Probes*. Minneapolis, Minn.: Bellwether Media, 2018.

ON THE WEB

FACTSURFER

Factsurfer.com gives you a safe, fun way to find more information.

1. Go to www.factsurfer.com.

2. Enter "Moon" into the search box.

3. Click the "Surf" button and select your book cover to see a list of related web sites.

INDEX

The images in this book are reproduced through the courtesy of: pratilop prombud, front cover; NASA/GSFC/Arizona State University/ Wikipedia, pp. 2, 7, 10-11 (Moon); Cameron Spencer/ Getty Images, pp. 4-5; Fisherss, pp. 6-7 (Earth); TuiPhotoEngineer, pp. 8-9 (Moon); NASA/ NASA Images, p. 9 (Earth); HelenField, p. 10; Fahad Sulehria / Stocktrek Images/ Alamy, pp. 12-13; kdshutterman, pp. 14-15; Michael Warwick, pp. 16-17; NASA / Neil A. Armstrong/ Wikipedia, p. 19; muratart, pp. 20-21.